CAMERA LYRICA

Winner of the 1999 Beatrice Hawley Award

Camera Lyrica

■ ■ ■

poems

AMY NEWMAN

Alice James Books
Farmington, Maine

▪ Acknowledgements

Grateful acknowledgements are made to the editors at the following journals, in which some of these poems first appeared (although, in some cases, in different form and under different title): *The Carolina Quarterly, Colorado Review, The Connecticut Poetry Review, Denver Quarterly, The Gettysburg Review, Hayden's Ferry Review, The Ohio Review, Quarter After Eight, Riverwind, Willow Springs.*

Excerpts from *American Visions: The Epic History of Art in America* by Robert Hughes. Copyright ©1997 Alfred A. Knopf, New York. Reprinted with permission. Excerpt from "Introduction to These Paintings" by D. H. Lawrence from *Poets on Painters: Essays on the Art of Painting by Twentieth-Century Poets*, edited by J. D. McClatchy. Copyright © 1988 The Regents of the University of California. Reprinted with permission. Excerpt from *Arcadia* by Tom Stoppard. Copyright © 1993 by Tom Stoppard. Reprinted by permission of Faber and Faber Inc. Excerpt from "Enjoying the Forbidden Fruit" by Connie McCabe from *Saveur* magazine Sept./Oct. 1996. Reprinted with permission. Every attempt has been made to acquire permission for excerpts from other works. For unlisted excerpts, please see Notes, page 65.

Library of Congress Cataloging-in-Publication Data

Newman, Amy (Amy Lynn)
        Camera lyrica : poems / Amy Newman.
          p.   cm.
        ISBN 1-882295-24-2
        I. Title.
      PS3564.E9148C36 1999
811'.54—dc21   99-31438
                         CIP

Alice James Books gratefully acknowledges support from the University of Maine at Farmington and the National Endowment for the Arts.

Alice James Books are published by the Alice James Poetry Cooperative, Inc. University of Maine at Farmington 98 Main Street Farmington, Maine 04938.

I wish to thank the Illinois Arts Council for an Individual Artist Fellowship which aided in the completion of this book. I am grateful to those whose attention to the manuscript helped shape it: Tom Andrews, Peg Peoples, Barbara Jordan, Janet Kaplan, Wayne Dodd and Joyce Barlow Dodd.

All the unwritten belongs to Joe Bonomo.

For Joe

Contents

I pierced the body of [a kingfisher], and fixed it on the board; another wire passed through his upper mandible held the head in a pretty fair attitude, smaller ones fixed the feet according to my notions, and even common pins came to my assistance. The last wire proved a delightful elevation to the bird's tail, and at last—there stood before me the real *Kingfisher....*

—JOHN JAMES AUDUBON

Cezanne felt it in paint, when he felt for the apple.... He felt the sky-blue prison.

—D. H. LAWRENCE

Freedom cannot be conceived simply.

—FLANNERY O'CONNOR

I

...

Representation

The rib cage scales biology and architecture,
music and form. One breath, and the breadth

of the human shifts, and then idea, and then
egress, and never mind the science of skin.

The cage of bones breathes as a body, bends
like a day lily leaf and is all manner of supple

though bone is hard, this structure is both cover
and open, is net and wing. Ribs struck clean as keys.

The ribs like a corduroy curtain, and on the stage
a meaty heart a little shy. But what manner of thought is this

for such a little girl? The kindergarten teacher had a son
who left the riding mower running when it got stuck

on a rock wedged too sure in the wheel. Then it kept mowing
once he removed it, too quick, a surprise. This was

before the safety bar, a good invention,
this was the very early Sixties.

It was a tiny afternoon
in the most temporary of decades.

Travel Diary

Just like that, the opening
of an eye. An apprehension in the ascending lid,
deciding proportion, engraving.
The eye knows plainly inside, outside. *Last night
trees exhaled as if the breeze relieved them.* I'm feeling

disoriented into the land, its demanding roads
so ongoing, horizontal and trailing
like exhaust the beautiful sentences,
flat history flowering
in its cursive hand. *Trees exhale
and the leaves fall.* The eye's mute reference,

the character of travel,
presence opening into letters, and the now
becomes a trail of letters behind it like hair.
Last night the trees let go of leaves like exhaling,
relieved at this lessening, and the leaves
as fine scales in their shifting descended

their only distance, ideal their notion of journey
as in any travel diary. That's what I'm seeing,
I wrote, that's what I'm writing. As if

words plainly interested in their surroundings
record the entire: *Majuscule, Minuscule.*
I'm battered by the *last nights*,

and the *meanwhile* especially,
whose axis radiates like steam, whose axis
records ongoing. The eye opens or the eye closes,
the irresponsible, servile eye. Into the alphabet of the eye

the howling wilderness of letters, characters in a tract,
digging in at the heels.

Realism

This never happened: in a kind of a sleepwalk, the painter
outlines his body on paper, proposes
to engage the physical world. To study God's parcelling out
of beauty and the flat back distance
of American history. Later, the paper

is blank. Still later, the outline
returns. The influence is Time—
impossible to make of the present a narrative,
to trace the material world as it rehearses
again and again its vestigial shape, to describe

the duplicate of life, more than estimate
the mortal substances as they are delicate, precise,
and in each other's arms, all blood and ornament
sexing like caterpillars
beneath the century's velvets.

This happened: the Realist Charles Wilson Peale
unearths a story of the natural world
made suddenly retrospective, the fossil
of a mastodon in upstate New York.
Now, was the West beautiful,

or full of terror? Is the bluebird's eye
the color of a saint's apprehension near a patch
of moonlight done as marrow? Peale arranged the bones
in a vast room, celebrants beneath the rib cage with cocktails
as if beneath the vaulting of the promise

of America. Her red mouth open.
Not history's likeness but the very thing,

canopied as the dare of archeology.
All of the time-arts
love/hate time. Still later, Venus hides her sex

behind all the adjectives describing the drape
of an artist's handkerchief.
Her small foot shows beneath, prompts
a frenzy of verisimilitude. For how could we
in truth behold her? Against heavenly white

and the world's water green, this reticent girl
in rich oils, hidden in the field
of what I imagine: the rose of her flesh,
veiled skeleton, all that subtle, tense
taut bone. And its interior:

a planetary, incomprehensible blue.

The Vulnerable

In the wasp's lineage from filament to airplane:
some grip of distance, some idea of thrust,

wicked thinness into the head wind,
hot little jaw and lifted shell.

In the earth's line from pitch to ground:
its dark address, the wells so deep they hold

like valentines the immaterial.
Delicate as secrets are the physical sciences,

dense and rare is the world's flipped skirt,
with a great wind basting and stirring its hem,

and underneath, the heart's content,
a crest of jewel, all latitude,

or its opposite:
a kind of homesickness, a disenchantment.

Group Photograph Before the Hydrangeas

Centered and focused, the people rail dissonant
before the hydrangeas, soldiers of process
in the afternoon flash. Pale and thoughtful
secrets of congenital blooms, ingenious
and panting a warm sticky pink,
crescendo of idea in a lake of day.

The flowers are pretending to be
asleep: their idea of focus is
one last long boat gliding out; the latent suck
of water to the root; a flower or gang of flower
petals, obscure and certain sprout of color.
The people are quite lucid by comparison.

What camera pretends to know its
roots as spy-glass, tilted and refracting a magnified perception,
the soft shades of purple prismatic, the lucid and livid
faces an adhesive and difficult corsage?
Spiky tiny teeth and high relief.
Ugly blossom gathered at the stems, passive
and proud, wide-open.

Hydrangeas vocal as the summer,
and dark as candy at the core of blossom
agree with all the wind by feeling sleepy. A lick
of thick cohesive perfume lures
the noses and the rooty mouths
of the stick figures, compassionate and inarticulate.

Flesh

This evening we may press together hands
until they form a steeple made of flesh.
The night's so cold the lake's a frozen wafer
and though the air might make us cold, the blood
insists that all that moves is holy
and so, all of us moving are the church.

On Sundays there are chairs for us in church,
we dip into clear water our human hands,
the basin carved from marble, veined and holy
and then the now-cleansed body curves its flesh
into an S shape, rigid body, mobile blood
that, through the thinnest skin, through wafer-

thin, has veins as blue as what we wait for.
That is a magic worth its price in church—
no sheepish rabbit but a cup of blood,
no flourish of a dove like clapping hands
but one round thought, a coin of flesh,
to mark the presence of the very holy.

A priest I knew looked physically so holy
I lapsed into desire for the real world, the way for
my own longing: I longed to lick his neck, that flesh
was nearly clear and I thought sex in church
would be a christening of sorts. I pictured hands
entwined as doves, a spray of water, pictured blood

that wept from statues to announce our mingling. Blood
would trumpet our new union, a fusion holy
and sanctified. Our town would fill with tourists, laying hands

upon my now-glimmering form, and he would go away for
a short time, return with tablets, build the new church.
No sin allowed. Some incense and hymns, to flesh

out the moneychangers; though they would be our flesh,
their lives were clotted with bad blood,
and this would be the new millennium, a church
aspiring to be simple, to be pure and holy
as we loved our bodies, stacked like wafers
with our blessed, clean, and active hands.

The doors of church are large so all the holy
may watch as miracle drinks blood and changes wafer
to flesh so sure you almost see His hands.

The Cruciferous Trees

1

The Roman cross inherits the body of the man
and places him upon it, in invisibility but visible
forever: a longer vertical, the shorter, horizontal branches
of this intended replication. And do you have a flourish,
the arms ending in a trefoil? The metal always
sprouting, both hands and head aflower,
a Christ bird flying hard out of its ribs.
If it can make productive this idea of the offspring,
if it can make essential a mark of all things blessed,
if out the garden window, the trees are shaped like crosses,
the art controls its love without the strings. Why bother?
A form can be a very tricky thing.

2

Order, in architecture; the column, three parts:
base, shaft, capital, with an entablature of
architrave, frieze, cornice. A company of threes,
a triad, a *triforium*, a tribute to the church.
Three birds have patterned outside on the lawn
among those cruciferous trees, curled
into smooth stone figures in this rain, their feathers
nearly herring-bone. One bird will wing away in some small terror,
whipping like a Saxon vane, a figure fleeing
from the Middle Ages. Then, how radiant the image:
the way they painted all the statues
to imitate true life and gild it very brightly.

Proverbial

His hair vicuña-short, suede bristle-brush,
against and past the small steel oval, a camel tries first
his shoulder, because like us, from the head, he feels
the slimmest there. Grasshopper's arm'd go
right through, though one false move and it'd
snap. Off. Not much give in a wiry frame.

Back to the camel, it's common knowledge
the hump's the trouble. How that droll eye
would study the non-space, regard this life
as that one thirst. Less water! Less water!
And heaven might be one long drink.

Like horsehide, camel hair is dreamy. Muscle-dusty,
fragrant, a curry comb whirls up a small
Sahara cloud above the sweat. The camel
peers through the eye, and squints to see
the other side: same thing. *Like caramel,*
I'll ease around it. His hooves too split
to hold thin steel. The point was

the ascent up through the eye, a ghost-like thing,
diaphanous. Because a camel's eyes
are side-set, *I couldn't even see the thing!*
He wishes he were smooth, like vowels,
friction through a stream of air surrounded (sometimes)
by some letters. In vowel, there is
camel realized, buoyant, now ascendant
in the *a*, the *e*.

A Minor Hymn to the Eucharist

Purity of posture. Whosoever accepts sexually
love's slight crisp taste and the febrile grace
—like all of heaven's animals except the cat, whose whiplike tail

delineates the absence of denial—whosoever
transfers wafer to the lush of soft, crescent of
flesh, a categoric passion of absorption....

She or he receives the blessing of idea,
the most, most literal, the atmosphere of ecstacy and ecstacy,
the text of *text*. Not solely one parent of a dear good child

but blessed miracle, and that real parent
against a scrim of rye and wheat, of scrod and salmon,
the ceremony of translation, when the vast mirage washes out

to the literal city behind it, its corset of symbol, dress of the real.
It happens: We charm the gesture into miracle, eat
the miracle at the font of grace,

and then we dine on grace.
We are become translations, declensions,
enameled and spread open like a clean filet,

each flake of us washed white. In a little town
a pan of rice and milk and sugar boils to a thick paste,
some kind of ritual cooled to a sweet frost.

And all the cows are bathed and scrubbed,
and hung with flowers, and when it's time,
each dense, elaborate animal may stir and plod

to a fat bowl of quiet, chaste imagining,
sugary with grace, and sup as the confectionery presence
gilds the marrow and the milk with intense dreaming.

Plates 1—15

So that was when there was a *lifting*;
and the idea of a god was a: *beacon in the wilderness.*
And the *blessed* had their reward *over the ways of the earth.*
So the restless face of *the Jesus figure* was like a window in a rain
that through which sight is *restored* and also
buffed and *polished to a fine gloss* that is indistinct
and this will be imagined
and this a certain kind of clarity....

How *unfair* the world would become
how covered though with a *beauty of lichen*
and a towering of fruit *loved* by the insects
like muscular parcels of industry,
the silent *scrutiny* of the animals, of the peacock
whose flesh was supposed to have been *incorruptible*
and a sense in spite of itself
that this will be our unhappy *paradise.*

The presence of angels was said to have been
unprecedented; *it was a memory* of realism
that gave the people a sense of emphasis
spreading a margin, making *the field*
full with objects christened and recognized.
And maybe the divine can be discovered in the most
unlikely places, such uncertainty
full on with splendor.

Some of the painted Madonnas bear a likeness to Venus,
a dangerous craving for mere beauty. Was this
the end of the pagan world? Were these

angels embracing the representatives of mankind,
to stand for all sustained by grace? A lifting—
the delicate rose palisade of wings,
each painted, archéd foot; angelic insteps float
out of the wilderness, ascending to the pretty world.

Painting the Assumption

Not hard to imagine, anymore, the world a circle of virtuals,
    that one day the Virgin will be,
right in front of us, assumed. Her day won't begin
      in the usual way, instead of just waking and making the coffee
she finds herself glinting a bit, like her skin is too smooth
    —her face shimmers if she moves too fast. Maybe,
she thinks, she's slept too well, as her feet press
    far lighter into the floor. By the time she's at market,
surveying the wines, her clothes are slack, and in front of the neighbors
    she lifts, this long-legged woman, superior, incomparable,
radiant, her head upturned like the brim of a chalice,
    the grocery sack a brown paper wing,
inside it all cotton, cotton.
    Stepping from a bath, a woman
rises. Her damp hair might begin
    singing beneath the towel. It's in the kitchen
the movement begins, but she doesn't ascend from her plinth-like heels.
    Sideways the kitchen revolves, the white counter
grows flecks and parabolas, grayish and pink,
    and the food merges restlessly back to something
bubbling ecstatic through the oven's glass door.
    What looked like a Christmas tree slows to be
clear green and clear pink pliant containers
    so supple with food, and near-near-genius
while in the next room over mounds of this stuff,
    women chirp and sparkle, elastic, *oh blessed ladies*
of the cul-de-sacs, of don't let the screen door slam,
    six ounces of white milk in a jelly glass,
the marvel of bread crumbs, of tinned fish,
    a teaspoon of dry scarlet wine in the gravymaster,
sweet house of frost-free refrigeration, telephones
    ringing into air in an empty kitchen, and

no one to answer it, years until anything's made
     to insist on this doubling of body clicking a voice
into silence, this kind of a sacristy kitchen,
     its lawn brisk and clipped, its damp towels drying.
In art, how is the motion captured? One wash of the brush and
     a grocery sack here, the oranges tumbling happily.
Too much idea makes the happy room Jello.
     The paint would have to be pinks and yellows,
fruits and canned foods, a sheen for the slipcovers
     plastic in August. Some dark, vivid hues
will bring them all back.

Putting to Bed an Acre

Of a cotton blanket I breed buildings in my sleep.
The singular Egyptian line, drawn like ordinary time
my half-note down it,
the lintel from the Greek across,
a hat, a roof, a meaty sky.
The semicircle Roman arch as pure as air,
I shape a salmon's flexing tip to tail.
Did the night plan this sky in layers
like a sweet cooked filet? Does the estate
assume a person, the cemetery's

swollen gum of earth across the street,
and sore fresh teeth shot forth?
The excess of beauty, the weight
of the body's decorative idea exhales in bed
like a sea creature
moving in pulses. I let the flowers
go unwatered. I watered them into the ground.
I wore the flowers on a print dress,
I watched a flower bloom
on film, a stingy bud that changed its mind,

and pulled in like a folding letter,
flip, flip, flip, dear mother, dear aunt,
inside click-clacking,
the sugary paper soft thin bone.
I fold myself brisk as semaphore,
skin vellum-feminine, rectangle of girl,
a game of solitaire in a little house
where blatant walls support a roof,
withstand its pressing down.

Interior I

A snail's shell, so elaborate, its literal
cunning

Her body moves from the bed toward
the window

and tiny, hiding against an entire beach
but not so here in this hand, and I
in this house

The light collapses
over her left shoulder

the pearly hard and delicate devils.
What random. What negative love

The town across the river will seem to
rise slightly as the camera
pulls back
and left

of its body into a small hardness
like a dream of a shell

Rising

nothing to compare it to

On the top of the hilltown: a tiny cow,
a tiny horse
Beyond which lies the ocean

II

All birds arriving at a tree
at once, like a conclusion

Out the window
a tiny horse
moves out of frame

in their tendency towards grace

Darkening, lessening of sunlight

Blue Cranes civilize the plain
in a repeated pattern,
all wing and glide in smooth pale white
like a settlement of churches,

Random birds fly by the window
approx. fifty feet away
Can we get them to land?

I have some words in the vertical

Cut to

that are desperate and lost in our horizontal

Her pale throat and the opening
of blouse, white, at her neck Cut to

that dragon of endless arrangings
and minutes accumulating in shiny scallops
extravagant scales

Full shot: the bed and the window
She walks into frame, falls back,

of a rough faith, a shiny sea, a war of ships
in a storm

eyes closed?

Your sex taut and frilled like a Sampan

III

Exterior shot: a fairly smooth sea
many small boats, of the Chinese type
known as Sampans
Sunny day

No, dark clouds in foreground. Rain
and choppy water.

Sounds: squawk of water birds, of water

Action: Men unloading shabby cartons
to dock. Some haste in approaching

storm. Too many birds in the scene.
A tiny horse

In Medias Res

The unpredictable and the predetermined unfold together
to make everything the way it is....It's the best possible time to be alive,
when almost everything you thought you knew is wrong.
— VALENTINE, IN TOM STOPPARD'S *ARCADIA*

I'm haunted and awake into the skin,
alone against the windows and the middle
of the night, concerned with Michelangelo,
his back upon the scaffold, the Sistine Chapel perfect
but his *Pietá*, unfinished. The tempera brushing placid

at the temper of the sky, the angels
and the scale of mortal reach and God
in tandem, this course of our unfolding.
An echo in a church envelops like requiem.
Did Mozart really write his in the middle of his dying?

I may not know my own Jerusalem—I might arrive
much in the midst, to fidget feminine or quick,
a kind of sparrow above the rushing water,
too small to span the cool cement Niagara
of this century's teenage core, as Natalie Wood

in *Splendor in the Grass,* that kind of love,
unfinished. Let's say all of us might run
across a field of middle distance
in her coltish clumsy way, like a foal,
like she did, in the middle of the picture

toward her parents, simultaneously
to the future and the past. I wanted her
to let that sprint describe itself into adulthood,
leave her safe from movies such as *Inside Daisy Clover.*
Have I recognized the text, my thin heritage,

my worry? I never can sleep; it's like waking up
in the Sistine Chapel. We see
on the ceiling, the hands nearly touch.
Here is our stretch, our almost.
This is our taste, our equidistance.

II

■ ■ ■

Darwin's Unfinished Notes to Emma

Actually Darwin's gradual loss of faith, which he downplayed
for fear of upsetting his devout wife Emma, had...complex causes.
—RICHARD DAWKINS

The world this morning is wide as this sea,
and full of potential. I think of you so often,
with great sadness at our distance.

        ▪

Some of the plants I see are extraordinary. One,
whose petals seem lined with cream
and opens out so full
reminds me of your hands...

        ▪

It is a diverse world, Emma, the structure
is breathtaking. We will never unlearn these

hours of facts. The world...

        ▪

I think of you especially as we observe the orchids,
those flowers that you so admire. I would like to give you
all the varieties of orchid

        ▪

Bees cut holes and suck the nectar
at the bases of certain flowers, which,
with a very little more trouble, they can enter

at the mouth

        ∎

The mistletoe depends on birds to spread its seeds, the
flowers depend on insects, it is all
a series of increasingly apparent
relationships. Nature moves
in profitable steps.

To propagate, the orchid,
I am flustered to write,
requires the cooperation
of the male wasp, and so resembles

        ∎

we have acquired some idea of the lapse of time;
the mind cannot grasp the full meaning of the term
of even a million years

        ∎

Do you remember that one morning I smelled of nectar?
Darling, the world is feral, and we are natives.

        ∎

Of all the species of bee,
only the humble-bee can visit the common red clover.
It has to do with curvature, with length
of the proboscis, too slight
to be appreciated by us. Whole fields of red clover

offer in vain their abundant supply
of nectar to any other bee. This idea

of a vast spread of fresh green waiting
with all its juice,

■

Instinct! The mental processes of animals!

■

To propagate, the orchid
requires the participation of

the male wasp, to get the pollen
on his legs, and to get him to transfer

the pollen to other orchids.
The orchid must resemble genitalia,

a female wasp, her body,
so the insect will copulate

with the flower. The orchids had to become
desirable, so this man wasp

will alight from one to another,
cross-pollinating. She wears her color

like flesh, and scents brazenly
for him: spreading herself in the cooler air;

her sweet interior; the fumbling
of the dizzy wasp. This did not happen

as a whim. This is
an extremely intricate subject.

■

The similar framework of bones in the hand of a man,
wing of a bat,
fin of the porpoise,
leg of the horse

■

I am remembering your subtle throat, how in the heat
your skin will almost pearl. Underneath your dress of skin
all that fragile blood. You are this morning

a field of clover, and I feel drawn to this,
a humble-bee. I am carried in the world's
mouth

■

The same pattern in the wing and the leg of a bat,
in the petals, stamens, and pistils of flowers

■

This is a matter of perfection, over time,
and complication. Did the orchid have the means
to think itself into seducing, to adapt as idea
the perfect dress of reproduction,
the female wasp

a bit of fur and soft petal
curved like its soft parts

■

Last night a dream: you and I dusted in pollen

■

I would like to believe

Naturalism

If he could preserve the natural world,
it will always seem beautiful: corpses
of flesh like modeling clay, his own form
stiffening as the bird flares, he spread each wing,
a sexless flight, or flightless sex. He loved

the ugly argument of vast biology's
bent head flexed by drama, blood, the fragile skin
tumescent. It is a luxury to dress the infinite in feathers,
to note the blind unholy drives
on printing plates, and all the world

America. We must consider it
redemption—in spite of the scattering offspring—
the pace of his work as he wired bird to board.
Audubon worked, that he might preserve
the beautiful bird in a pose most alive,

(to animate the language of pursuit, of hunt,
the gift of feather), to wrest it of its sky-blue prison
to the land thought pure and clean beneath us.
By the end of this poem, there should have been
some sense of beauty in the sound of birdshot,
a taste in the mouth like blood, and grace, a warmth
of the small bird body. The swallow-tailed kite
is a glorious blue.

Audubon studied shape as shape, all that attracts
the hunter. Everything leg and wing
in the physics of our wilderness.
In its landscape of beautiful curves lives
the arc of the kingfisher, wishing the world

would not find it so beautiful,
its wings balanced, and weighing between them
the heft of the invisible: God
and indifference, blind as erection
and tremendous, tremendous.

Adam's Dream

The Imagination may be compared to Adam's dream—he awoke and found it truth.

— JOHN KEATS

He dreamt airy clouds with the whites of eye

He dreamt beasts larger than himself and smaller than himself

He dreamt caterpillars upon whose length of fur the winter was
    predicted

He dreamt dresses falling with the ease of water from waists and backs

He dreamt elements packed into squares, abbreviated

He dreamt force and density and velocity

He dreamt generals and generalizations, guns and gravity

He dreamt harbors; he dreamt of harbors

He dreamt into the center of his own dreaming

He dreamt just paragraphs: restful, sweet rooms of words

He dreamt kindergarten and kindergarten tables

He dreamt loss. Here he nearly stopped dreaming.

He dreamt *more like a man / flying from something that he dreads /
than one Who sought the thing he loved.*

He dreamt not what you'd expect: not Nature, though it was all
    around him

He dreamt of the sound of things put together from letters

He dreamt peacocks dragging tails like suns

He dreamt questions followed by question marks, then
    all the punctuation

He dreamt reason and passion, the harness and the horse

He dreamt, straining credulity in the 20th Century

He dreamt the tiny, the magnificent

He dreamt ululation

He dreamt valium into being, and then out of being

He dreamt wild things tamed

He dreamt x-chromosomes
He dreamt y-chromosomes
He dreamt zodiacal light; this woke him.

Penelope's Notes to Orpheus

1

This wet land is a weird equation, the lily's
anther bowed with pollen, the lily's stigma
reaching, and all around them,
moths, who beat their gray, ecstatic wings.

2

At the moment you saw her gone,
the world as fair as any wager and her, blooming
like a crazy vine;
it did you up. I tremble

at your impossible body. I consider you as one
defining loss, its difficult glass
curtain. I want to say, Orpheus,
are you as bad as I hope? Could you

have maybe been playing your music
to me? I feel remote
as any island. Some days I look out on
the water's turned back,

and no ship can cross it, no matter
how famous the man.

3

A moth is dusting his legs
in a flower: impossible weight, his
vague gray lust; the bloom and he
nearly graze the ground. I promise you something

you'd shape a sound on,
white as a page but full, of little
pointed licks and volutes. How close to the earth
can we hover? You would fill me like a sail.

Sophistry of the Quince Fruit

The Garden of Eden, so the story goes, was in Mesopotamia,
near native quince territory. Since apple supposedly originated in Central Asia,
chances are good that the forbidden fruit was actually a quince.
     —CONNIE MCCABE

Modesty ruled childhood. In book and magazine,
the lovely body was left to those
who couldn't account for it: their hair, their eyes,
their education, all smooth and easy to believe.
The shimmer of my neighbor against a dinner plate,
the beauty of their clothes and cuticle, according to
McCall's Girl's Guide to Beauty and Glamour,
a bearable example of random chance. I learned

to manicure: the little grin of steel
abraded tiny moons. The curves composed themselves
to generate more curves, so everywhere was roundness, spheres,
and bows, loops and circles, echoing my fingertips?
Some girls had skin that pearled with grooming tips.
My body sank into a boy's slim hips and wilderness.
The sloping of my backyard loved my descent,
consoled me, a prairie of my own botanic muddle,

a charm school of silviculture
flowering insensible: the lilies to my hips,
fur of asparagus going to seed, and after dusk all heads,
all blossoms, downturned, unassuming.
How awkward was this child. And all the others
like her: tame-quiet, plain and common.
Enveloped by the fruit trees and brushwood, and perfumes
that closeted an Eden. Eve gave us trouble, evinced
all this clutter, her body that curve we were meant to become.

In my backyard's recess of chestnut, and rhubarb,
some quince trees dissembled; harrowing shoots pointing
back to the sky. I blame it on quince fruit,
their gold little bellies and smug cicatrices,
their slithery leaves and the casual way they
grow cool at night. How like a motif
hang those tiny full moons, round pungent fruit,
shameless, crisp, bitter engines of failure.

Barbie at Forty

likes the title applied, like lipstick, in
one garish stroke. Her eyeliner wit, she
christened with Ken, the last time she saw his
molded behind. He's working out

his physical form. *I've got this Corvette,*
I've got these shiny legs,
she'd think to herself in the Sixties, when
dresses were scratchy and beautiful,

like the itchy black number she'd wear
at the microphone, hot little matchstick with
one lengthy leg crossing the other, pink
and thirsty as frosting, the ache of it.

Now all's quiet with her, and the rhythm,
so helpful, her walk, as patent as toast,
let her down like her strings fell and she was
a marionette, weird puppet, spilled milk,

so nobody cry then, okay? Okay.
Vexing doll, played all drunk like a mother,
all dormant, inanimate, feminine call,
she's done flexing and sheening, like that hootch

rubber Francie, and finding her own body's
hollow return, she nestles synthetic
and loves her own counterfeit restlessness,
blowing out candles and finally sexing.

The Sentimental Side of Girls

This is about flat planes and
natural resources. This poem's subject
is that and angles.
Put on a sanded oak top some stain.
Put on a red oak stain.

Red oak stain follows the grain.
Red oak stain is a forced cheeriness.
Wood grain embraces both vertical and horizon,
as a sunset is horizontal and rising.

Wood grain points to the left or right
tells on the tree how old and what.
Sanding makes wood a friend and smooth.
Lakes are surrounded by unfriendly trees.

Trees are convinced of the vertical distinction.
They have more sense than to think horizontal.
Lakes are blue and lie on their sides,
and love horizontals with their languishings.

Romantic Gestures

One pressed me against a white oak,
its branches preparing to hand down the evening,
lengthening like my shoulder blades the possibilities
of that intersection between normal

and beautiful. This quiet day surprised by intrusion,
a front door's insistence on the outside,
wide as anyone's comprehension of it,
beautiful as a dress, and the tree

was a way of speaking, and up through the limbs
hung a distance of blues and whites.
What else should I remember? There were blooms
whose petals felt like flesh,

the flesh of a hand, or a mouth, petals
cream at the tip, their desperate move
toward the sepal, the ovary, that
fevered the cream to a pink; but still,

What white oak? What afternoon?
The body's inability to be a part
of the popular world. So, I would like to say,
so, I let the dress fall open,

I let go of my dress, we opened the dress
together, as if uprooting flowers,
as if for a moment its pattern of dogwood
began a bloom, and now the landscape

was inside it, this ceremony
of the dress, how it could become
a little diaphanous threshold
against the rational world of things.

Violets

Im Kampf zwischen dir und der Welt sekundiere der Welt.
—FRANZ KAFKA

Last on the lake. The cathedral doors close.
The gothic nave afrost. Did children, in their covering cloth,
skate stars across the clean
lavender ice, and toss sweet sugar? A long skirt's lace sieved flurried
    snow,
or did I dream the entrance glint and shimmer, some hush as night
achieved itself, a baby's rising chest? I remember
wanting the shade pulled as animals husked,
their light pads frisking the carpeted church.
I thought my hands were caught in blankets
whipped like cream, and that the smallest shift
would ruin all the cold with hot.

Or was I watching skaters? All heads turn, a rustling skirt,
the clock a pocket of time in a pocket. Figures pressed
    and patterned
likewise, a couple shushing left, right,
glide, hand in each other's patterned glove, her costume white,
his dark tuxedo folding, clapping. And to my eye, if I'm asleep,
an arc of patterned velvet, a bunch of flowers tied
like at their wrists. The glancing stems alight, ablaze,
fall into hands, accept upon their petal-faces

the declining snow. We all looked up.
And snow patterned us, like stage lights, each profile
fluttering candle-quiet. And not a snowy lake, but white,
white frosting, rich with crescents, iced purple, yellow, the flowers
wild underfoot in spring. Have you seen the little things?
We cut some slices of the lake, and served it,
yellow, yellow as a yolk. Some people love the taste of violets,

real ones, and perfume their mouths
as if the world were a blank white,
and they the fragrant stencils.

Scrub Pines

Seasons are full of it:
the buds return in a time they call
particular to a tree
or out of their dirt in the pushing green
a silent child in the corner.

Out by the beaches I see pictures
strands of sharp grasses lying on sand dune
I haven't been there. I know the scent
of dry leaves of blades withered
wings of rooting plants.

That child, she
has a bad Saturday.
She can't speak in the proper way.
She sees out her window the stones
of the cemetery, thinks
on that hill is a particular sound.

Mozart's Wife

was drying her hands in the bathroom,
although we didn't know who she was.
She'd had a difficulty with the machine through which
one pulls a linen towel, and said
how hot like language were the dryers.

She was vivid. She was exploding. She missed
also the linen of her youth, which was
a dearer weave, and so to her
it seemed that everything
was a sacrifice, and she should know.

The towel was like underclothes, she thought,
and when she spoke
I saw her mouth become a bird, so full, and then a fruit,
and then a plate of fruit, the act of a pear
ripening.

That says enough. And like her,
not enough. I met Mozart's wife in the bathroom
during intermission, and she was charming.
We all described our favorites: fabric, fresh leaves, the day
        at a lake.
Everyone has a story.

What the Maid Saw

If anything was out of place I'd wonder,
is he provoking me? The leaded ashtray
takes the sunlight and spreads it out,
entrance singular and exit, plural,
fanlike. In this way I multiply the sun,
and I repeat myself as well, the sound
reappearing far down my tiny throat
successive and quieting.

I take four walls each night
like aspirin, my mirrored room becomes a throat and I'm
inside it, the soft increase of my figure
duplicating undiminished into the angles.
Each day I dust the body of the house, each night

I sleep the throat.
The husband, I think,
will dust me and sleep me. A singular entrance and I
sing plurals, I become a fan out of my mouth. I saw

a little boy surrounded by his toys
like in a puddle of things, or,
if I were smarter, *his toys like spilt honey, and*
deliberate his father's walk—who moved
the beautiful heavy glass,

its shape attendant, finite, its tactile
weight consoling the spherical cut?
Whose bare truth, like glass,
splays the inane sunlight? An hour later,
who moves it?

September

The open room, the window, the detail of a bird; the little town,
the evenings, the story it becomes.
On the hill is a hospital.
In the hospital is bone.

Spare women trill pale lines,
their mouths a shape through which can pass
a spire, a church, a piece of cake.
White is a color brisk as women, sharp

as the beak on a tiny bird,
sharp to crack and peel like paper, spit
a seed, a pit, a bone. In this poem,
these words blocked out in neighborhoods,

you are reading the blankets, the desperate corners
of sheets neat as pages, white and trim.
The frame of the window, the frame of the bed.
September was furniture

upholstered in color, a dresser lined
with cut glass bottles.
Pale yellow, like the Czar's glass.
The clear green of a lily stem.

Here is your child and a book beside the bed. Good night, the
papery words, the letters holding hands, goodnight,
a skein soft as petals
that sink into the skin.

If I could make a necklace of this story,
with its dim September stars justifying the blue,
I would wrap you in a calm like a vertical song,

I would carry you up in its intricate rise.
We can't be surprised

that paper holds us. That all around you is white.
That birds too small
to sing you sing you.

Stations of the Cross

A line of thin yet full in spirit, overfull,
who move through the eye of the hallow needle,
who enter this door of church, this station.
The worries like camels hustle at the hitching post,
stample and snort beneath the snow, hooves press the new
    white
back to green. All's fine, and quiet, and pages fold
open and press a vicious crease
faces upturned and holy holy.

The dromedary envelopes of lace and sound.
Each heart a tiny burst of crimson,
coiled twigs and basketweave
the Crown of Thorns a blooming plant,
Venetian red, its leafy beat. Apostles hold their books
and sing. The statuary white as teeth, some kitten's mouth,
a head and feet, a miracle to bloom so sweet.

Mother cat cleans all the kittens in the church.
Paw by paw, flared like light
in rich little pads of food and wine. Thorns
sting beautiful the irresistible gap
of dry cracked pink pink pad.
The skin so fine,
the divine shine shows arrows

of artery rouged by love, this leading
to prayer, curled up to sleep
sweet kitten of a heart.
And *quiet, quiet, quiet.*

Metaphor, the Midwest

We mixed the land, the length and width of it
combined the dirt and fleshy thinking,
like the rest of it: not a person matched
the land's description, not a person made
the sound the bird takes underwing, private,
secret, land not looking, not listening.

That sound. A violation of the flock,
a tilt and whistle. Yet a bird's gauging
flow cuts beauty right above the tilled flats
without so much as memory, and when,
like patterned fabric, more than one bird follows,
all the sky hangs southward. The heat waves push
softly on the passive vegetation.

It's this impossibility of curve
that we are bonded to. One sky, like a
promise underlined, latitude of stalks
as vivid, splendid and severe punctuation.

■

What place is this that ceaselessly measures
its vast and tame expanse, decent and mitered,
but for that pale dendritic hush of elevation?
This ground that we are gradually tending.

And hover thin-skinned nights to try,
not doing, not undone, not yet. But all days
lend slim finds toward night, decrease their light
and let things rest, the smallest blades at rest.

■

Like nails on boards, like plaids, a fastening
or a passing through, a thought like cable
and a brisk moon, the filament all spread and cast,
the thimble of good dirt that it would take.

■

Line neverends the string the horizon tied,
string-like, plain to a wrist and the whole world
pulled tight as a gift. Or encircling a waist,
a round plain pink, what your mother'd wear

when she woke up the lonely skirts and pulled
a slim lash tight as she walked sidewalks new
with crushed glass, they were,
so in the A.M. all of the city
looked gifty. If not a string or belt then

maybe not a thing at all but a line
that rides the ground as a snake would if:
the snake were still and:
distant, dolphin, harsh, terrene.

As the evening withdrew its vote, the pails
would empty down their purples, holding in
the wet and distaff longing for the wind.
What would be mythical then? A baby
shoe, an ark, a puddle swift and hissing

at the dry. This unambiguous surrounding,
the distance, true and rectilinear,
its pale watch and the paler day.
Someone felt the land deserved its slim
sore glow, affective heart.

Beautiful Math

Problem / Solution

One day the body is half-empty with liquid, next day
half-full. We birdfeather in the oscillating heat.
Science dreams our comparable densities.
Science is the last circus draw. A rustled bed means
won't be here when you get here,
the mattress a formula for guessing at distance.
This white sheet, times its cicatrice,
can tell you when that train will pull in.

In lightheaded upwards from South to North,
the singer describes the air through her mouth, charts
her notions of proportion and design. She's an architect,
singing the degrees from here
to there. She's all at sea. Like a compass
I'm looking away. What's the name of that instrument,
held up to the stars, tells you
all is lost?

XY

About this time, the world reduces like a sauce
into numbers. Spare of skin like they don't need it,
thin as real desire. A line curved
like a swan's neck and then back again
equals one and one. Let X equal the spare bone,
the concave tongue.
Y follows X like a chaser.

You like a map's distance rendered
in numbers, clear as a row of bottles,
one square of elevated detail
to represent years of heat. If you felt lost,
you'd have to spiral your form into a bottle,

toss this helix
the greatest length away, in a windmill arc
of force and velocity.

True North

A sextant fixes in cross hairs the stars
who yield to the blue circumjacence
they hang in. A measuring tool in the shape of its subject.
My whole leg met yours in bed
at your ankle; that's how long
it's going to be before you come home.
After the song, there is

a gulf where the song was.
The body is a true interlinear,
a text like in the Jesus Stories, and the cross
we make on our bodies,
North South East West.

Rabbits

The bow's ear tight-tied look of the
dark-eyed things who run although
they know we are the ones
who spread cracked feed each afternoon
like wishing, a scattering of vows
at the large tree and further down,
where other trees were cut. We mark
with vagrant Pleiades the days and months
of this wood growth, this leaf descent, and rabbits
pushing to full size. The lawn's decision
was to slope down, to yawn an open place
at the far end, to lie down flat
and let the train echolocate our nights
to find us sleeping, and retreat.
(Beginning with the engine car it cuffs us,
takes our pulse then grows smaller, lessens,
makes itself remote.) When we walk the grass's distance,
the rabbits stop, and mark their time.

A Note on the Type

1

In the alphabet of the garden, the Creeper Nasturtiums
are calligraphic, writing summations
in tendrils and slants. The calculus of symbol
and the move to the real. As quick as you please,

the back yard imagines its very own
theory of color. More than a spoonful of crows
lift like stitches and drive the air, then change direction
and travel back, as the ox plows,

this motion tending toward the infinite.
The hummingbirds adore
the trumpets of the Scarlet Climber, dot each like an *i*
in a word with many vowels. I'm chastened by perennials,

as the crows half-irritate the cold blue scrim,
and staple down their legs to limbs, make
ugly basket nests for eggs.
But the bird's got a cursive tendency, it

distorts the afternoon so Sans serif,
so suddenly italic, so sulky, and,
at about four o'clock, the male of the species
looks much more beautiful, puffed,

its pigment not so much applied
as illustrated. The glyph for find: two stick legs,
a body, little wings. A bird, its shape,
can stand for anything.

[detail]

line 17: Sans serif a little bit about the words
won't tell it all. Serif's the fine line
that finishes off the main strokes, sustains the N,
the M, maybe to cut, to sketch,
to mark with a stylus into soft and fragrant clay,
easy to cut in stone, less easy with a pen.
To underline emphatically the influence of the letter.
Sans serif, in French,
without serif. Without that line,
that elegant reminder of the form. As if the letters aren't
quite sure. But here are some Sans serifs for
pronouncing: Antiqua Olive semi-bold,
Futura bold, Futura light.
Without that line they are divested,
a soft, sweet yielding mouthful,
swept like sandstorm, embryonic,
abundant Sans serif.

2

Here is what evening tells us mathematically:
the probability of morning
is incommensurate. We take to pacing,
hastening back and forth
embodying repetition just this one way.

This is the famous *night's amnesia*
defined in textbooks, but only felt as
some documentary script of the moment
such as the insistent Garamond, the beautiful *f* abiding,
its ampersand paused in the heft of air.

If we imagine that the world is characteristically linear,
if the axiom has a forward property, then we conceive
by a series of words the infinite, sturdy
as Bembo Antiqua, or lucky and beautiful Lithographia, her
curled and quiet hair.

All our pacing is like commencement,
is our true rhythm, like early planting:
boustrophedon, wretched plowing, broken soil,
hard and fat hooves, and the farm
now freshly seeded, fully scented.

Come the fall we will be tugging at the remnants,
the erratic arugula, that delicious mistake.
Savoring the crisp and sinister green leaves
all irregular, all holy, that were like effulgence, shining forth, and
in the aftermath we wondered,
should we have a child?

[detail]

line 18: *Boustrophedon* as the ox plows,
while planting, and literally,
back and forth, a bovine pacing, just indelicate enough
to hear footsteps stamping on the roots:
bous from the root *gwou–*,
eventually, bull, cow, bovine, ox. Strophe,
from *strebh–* to wind, to turn, to make
a monkey of yourself with indecision.
· The lines we solely read from left to right
refrain from boustrophedon's sweet return,
left to right, then *right to left*, its
hebraic flushing of the characters,
a pacing and a swallowing,
boustrophedon most likely thinks
of swallowing all that it thinks.

3

So there I stood, just semi-bold,
and at the window, some small secretary to my life,
and sometimes, stationary. We have this pregnant land
that every evening heaps upon us its full summer.
It writes its lines on our failed skin
like insects, and insects
write upon us in near-terrifying pleasure.

And squirrels, and rabbits, nearly drunk
with skin-love, scratch the natural, leave
cracked shells and scattered shorthand.
The squirrels especially leave hieroglyphics,
markings cuneiform and ordered, like a cluster of stars
just spilled on a stomach, and in their emptying ink
a pool of radiant mistakes.

We are to each other that singular dispatch
that until now has left us fresh and cool at morning.
And are we only to behold each other,
or to make of us more formal markings?
Like any alphabet it is the grouping that makes sense,
though any letter left alone
will stand quite beautiful, though spare, though far too spare.

[detail]

line 11: hieroglyphics from the Greek,
hieros = holy, glyphein = to chisel.
A holy chisel, sacred and engraving, this one moment at night
when all the fields are planted and the evening animals,
the night ones, what are they called? come padding out from bushes,
husk their claws and mark expansion
merely by their being. And we're supposed to know, to calculate,
how much, and then how many, to watch as
in a line, great black and tapered crows
blossom like negative numbers.
No questions: tell me, let's expand the night
into some twenty years, we might become
a liquid, labial conversation of our bodies
pulled and engraving like a candy or a vine,
and this identity italic and intertwined,
undone and rising like moveable type.

The facts of manuscript making, the reproduction
made by lip and tongue a faint idea,
and by your hearty quill the rational
fattens real. At night, one of two things:
a little festival of birds flutters by the yard, sweet Baskervilles,
or it's a gathering, a fearsome thing,
of dark and rude bold wings, and incoherent: in this case,
squeeze a lemon, and take the juice,
gently, on a toothpick. Write
something, and as the citric past is all absorbed
into the paper, offer the present tense as gift.
And when the paper's dry, hold it above a flame,
ligatures stubborn as mistakes, and stiff
as private braille, as wedding cake.

Bringing Desire to the Fields

The farmer makes love to his wife in the field
to impress the achromatic land, to undo
its sullen mood. He's chosen a late afternoon,
and under the vast return of the crows
and under the imagined shade, the region's cool firma
is their *terra incognita*. They've walked forty steps down
past the Allis Chalmers. Out to reimagine
the cusp of season, the nuptial knot.

As yet there are no leaves upon the trees
to rustle, no vegetation spreading
like caprice across the fields.
What is this unfeasible something,
this stem of wish, this weird appetite?
Just yesterday the children shook like they were
made from sugar, and something wrote

words into his dream, to *fill the land with your
geography*. He's afraid his mind's too tired
from working the ungiving acres. What's to lose?
He sees now where her cotton dress
becomes a brook stream in this light, the air
as thin as kitchen breeze. Her body
a brook trout. Their acreage uncircumscribed.

Reader, I may have fallen
in love with the farmer. The hills beyond the couple
baffle themselves slowly. What a world
to want to run after. This promise
back to the garden. His thoughts while they are resting.
She's only imagining, stalks of yellow

flowers flush and frilled and rippling, and a song
of hours. On this and all the world's resources,
she lingers, lit up like a votive.

▪ *Notes*

The epigraphs for the book: Robert Hughes' quotation is from *American Visions: The Epic History of Art in America* (Knopf, 1997). Flannery O'Connor's quotation is from the introduction to *Wise Blood* in *Three by Flannery O'Connor* (Signet, 1962). D. H. Lawrence's quotation is from "Introduction to These Paintings" in *Poets on Painters: Essays on the Art of Painting by Twentieth-Century Poets*, edited by J. D. McClatchy (University of California Press, 1988).

The epigraph for "Travel Diary" is taken from Hughes' *American Visions.*

"Realism": the stories of Peale's thrill at discovering and supporting the excavation of the Mastodon skeleton are found in Hughes' *American Visions.* The trompe l'oeil painting described at the end of the poem is "Venus Rising from the Sea—A Deception [After the Bath]" by Peale's son, Raphaelle Peale.

The title of "A Minor Hymn to the Eucharist" is taken from the letters of Flannery O'Connor, in *The Habit of Being* (Farrar, Straus, Giroux, 1979). Though cats are considered by some unable to enter heaven, the cat in the poem knows otherwise. I am indebted to Elizabeth Coatsworth's book *The Cat Who Went to Heaven* (Macmillan, 1930) for this possiblity. The cow-bathing and feeding ritual described at the end of the poem is held at the beginning of the Tamil month of Thai throughout Tamil Nadu, India. A description of this festival is recorded in *Saveur* magazine (#10, January 1996).

"Darwin's Unfinished Notes to Emma": the epigraph and the information about the orchid can be found in *River Out of Eden* by Richard Dawkins (Basic Books/HarperCollins, 1995). Some lines in the poem are comprised partially of Darwin's own work, *The Origin of Species* (Norton, 1979).

"Naturalism": the story of Audubon's artistic and naturalistic drives is found in Hughes' *American Visions.*

The epigraph to "Adam's Dream" is from *Letters of John Keats* (Oxford University Press, 1947). The italicized lines are from William Wordsworth's "Lines Composed a Few Miles above Tintern Abbey."

"Penelope's Notes to Orpheus" : there is no evidence that Penelope was aware of Orpheus' plight, though the poem assumes otherwise.

"Sophistry of the Quince Fruit": the epigraph and a history of the quince fruit are found in *Saveur* magazine (#14, September/October 1996).

"Violets": the epigraph by Kafka translates: "In the struggle between yourself and the world you must take the side of the world," and is from Malcolm Bradbury and James McFarlane's *Modernism* (Viking, 1992).

"Mozart's Wife" is dedicated to Carolyn Highland, who had the dream.

"Bringing Desire to the Fields": Jung's account of a farmer and his wife associating their instinctual energy with that of the land is recounted in Thomas Moore's *The Re-Enchantment Of Everyday Life* (Harper Collins, 1996).

65

▪ Recent titles by Alice James Books

Amy Dryansky, *How I Got Lost So Close To Home*
Eric Gamalinda, *Zero Gravity*
Laura Kasischke, *Fire & Flower*
Janet Kaplan, *The Groundnote*
Celia Gilbert, *An Arc of Sorts*
B. H. Fairchild, *The Art of the Lathe*
Lisa Sewell, *The Way Out*
Sharon Kraus, *Generation*
Adrienne Su, *Middle Kingdom*
Ellen Doré Watson, *We Live in Bodies*
Kinereth Gensler, *Journey Fruit*
Cynthia Huntington, *We Have Gone to the Beach*
Nora Mitchell, *Proofreading the Histories*
Ted Deppe, *The Wanderer King*
Robert Cording, *Heavy Grace*
Forrest Hamer, *Call & Response*
E. J. Miller Laino, *Girl Hurt*
Doug Anderson, *The Moon Reflected Fire*
Deborah DeNicola, *Where Divinity Begins*
Robert McCann, *Ghost Letters*

Alice James Books has been publishing exclusively poetry since 1973. One of the few presses in the country that is run collectively, the cooperative selects manuscripts for publication through competitions. New authors become active members of the press, and participate in editorial decisions. The press, which holds both regional and national competitions, was named for Alice James, sister of William and Henry, whose gift for writing was ignored and whose fine journal did not appear in print until after her death.

Camera Lyrica was set in Adobe Bembo, a typeface based on the types used by Ventian scholar-publisher Aldus Manutius in the printing of *De Aetna*, written by Pietro Bembo and published in 1495. The original characters were cut in 1490 by Francesco Griffo who, at Aldus' request, later cut the first italic types.